THE

NDIAN CLUB EXERCISE.

WITH

EXPLANATORY FIGURES AND POSITIONS.

𝔓𝔥𝔬𝔱𝔬𝔤𝔯𝔞𝔭𝔥𝔢𝔡 from 𝔏𝔦𝔣𝔢;

ALSO, GENERAL REMARKS ON

PHYSICAL CULTURE.

ILLUSTRATED

WITH

ORTRAITURES OF CELEBRATED ATHLETES, EXHIBITING GREAT MUSCULAR
DEVELOPMENT FROM THE CLUB EXERCISE, ENGRAVED FROM
PHOTOGRAPHS, EXPRESSLY FOR THIS WORK.

_____

By SIM. D. KEHOE.

_____

British Library Cataloguing-in-Publication Data
A catalogue record for this book is available from the
British Library

Indian Clubs

'Indian clubs', or 'Iranian clubs' belong to a category of exercise equipment used for developing strength, and in juggling. In appearance, they resemble elongated bowling-pins, and are commonly made out of wood. They come in all shapes and sizes however, ranging from a few pounds each, to fifty pounds, and are commonly swung in certain patterns as part of exercise programs. They were often used in class formats, predominantly in Iran, where members would perform choreographed routines, led by an instructor; remarkably similar to modern aerobics classes. Despite their name, 'Indian clubs' actually originated in ancient Persia, Egypt and the Middle East, where they were used by wrestlers. The practice has continued to the present day, notably in the varzesh-e bastani tradition practiced in the zurkaneh of Iran. British colonialists first came across these eastern artefacts in India however, hence the name. The 'Indian clubs' became exceedingly popular back in the UK, especially during the health craze of the Victorian era. In a book written in 1866, by an American sports enthusiast, S.D. Kehoe, it was stated that 'as a means of physical culture, the Indian Clubs stand pre-eminent among the varied apparatus of Gymnastics now in use.' He had visited England in 1861, and was so impressed with the sport that he began to manufacture and sell clubs to the American public in 1862. They were used by military cadets and upper class ladies alike, and even appeared as a gymnastic event at the 1904 and 1932

Olympics. Their popularity began to wane in the 1920s however, with the growing predilection for organised sports. The modern juggling club was inspired by the 'Indian club' though; first repurposed for juggling by DeWitt Cook in the 1800s. He taught his step son, Claude Bartram to juggle with them, who later went on to form the first 'club juggling act'. Today, their popularity has been revived somewhat, by fitness enthusiasts who that they are a far safer means of excising, rather than the traditional 'free weight regimens'. Nostalgic replicas of the original clubs are still manufactured, as well as modern engineering updates to the concept, such as the Clubbell.

IMITATES ROWING PERFECTLY.

STROKE HARD AT THE BEGINNING.
EASY AT THE FINISH,
RECOVERY UNASSISTED

MACHINE FOLDED.

DESCRIPTION.

A cylinder made of brass, having a closed end and a highly polished interior, is placed in front of the oarsman, as shown in the illustration. The piston rod of the cylinder is connected with the short oars by means of a whiffletree and connecting rods.

The act of taking a stroke draws the piston away from the closed end of the cylinder, produces a vacuum, and the pressure of the atmosphere upon the piston simulates the resistance that is afforded by the water in rowing a boat. The cylinder (a sectional view of which is shown below), is provided with a series of small holes commencing about half way from the closed end, which allow the atmosphere to enter, and as the piston is drawn past them gradually relieve the vacuum. Hence the stroke is hard at the beginning, when the vacuum is perfect, and gradually becomes easier as these holes are passed. The air thus accumulated in the cylinder, finds free exit through a large opening in the closed end, as it is pushed before the piston in the "recovery." This opening is closed by a valve automatically upon the commencement of a new stroke. There is, therefore, neither *assistance* nor *resistance* to recovery. The oars turn so as to allow of feathering. Adjustable to any strength.

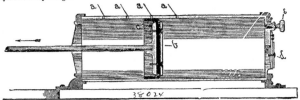

SECTIONAL VIEW OF THE CYLINDER.

a a a a.—Holes in the cylinder for the admission of air. As the piston is drawn past them, the vacuum is relieved.
b.—The piston.
c.—Leather cup or packing of the piston.
d.—Valve covering the large opening in the closed end of the cylinder. This valve closes automatically upon the commencement of a stroke and opens to allow free exit for the air accumulated in the cylinder as the piston is pushed back in the recovery.
e.—Screw filed away on one side, by unscrewing which a small or large opening is made, as described.

The machine will be sent to any part of the world on receipt of the price. In remitting send check on this city, postal money order, or by registered letter.

PRICE OF PARLOR MACHINE, $15.00.

NEW YORK, OCTOBER 28th, 1882.

DEAR SIR:—I have one of your PNEUMATIC PARLOR ROWING MACHINES, and find it the most perfect rowing machine I have ever tried. The motion is exactly like that of an oar, and the use of the machine will develop the same muscles that are called into play in rowing, and to the same extent. It is an excellent substitute for the water, and I gladly recommend it to professional and amateur oarsmen, and others. Hoping you will meet with the success you deserve, I remain, yours truly,
EDWARD HANLAN,
(Champion Oarsman of the World.)

GEORGE WILKES, Esq.

THE LOYAL GENTLEMAN, AND TALENTED EDITOR

OF

"WILKES' SPIRIT OF THE TIMES"

THIS WORK IS DEDICATED,

IN REMEMBRANCE OF MANY ACTS OF KINDNESS

SHOWN TO

THE AUTHOR.

CONTENTS.

INTRODUCTION.

GENERAL REMARKS ON PHYSICAL CULTURE.

INTRODUCTORY TO THE EXERCISES.

THE ALPHABET OF THE CLUB EXERCISE.

THE EXERCISES.

WITH ILLUSTRATIVE FIGURES.

EXERCISES FOR LADIES,

AND CONCLUDING REMARKS.

PECK & SNYDER'S MODEL AND POPULAR INDIAN CLUBS.

PECK & SNYDER'S MODEL INDIAN CLUBS.

The above Model Clubs are made of selected and seasoned maple and finely French polished, from 1 to 12 pounds.

Sizes	1 lb.	2 lbs.	3 lbs.	4 lbs.	5 lbs.	6 lbs.	7 lbs.	8 lbs.	9 lbs.	10 lbs.	12 lbs.
Per pair	$1 00,	1 25,	1 50,	2 00,	2 50,	2 50,	3 00,	3 00,	3 50,	4 00,	5 00.

PECK & SNYDER'S POPULAR INDIAN CLUBS.

These Clubs are made of maple, not fine polished, finished in wax, and quite as good for service as the finer finished.

Sizes	1 lb.	2	3	4	5	6	7	8	9	10	12
Per pair	75c.,	$1 00,	1 00,	1 25,	1 50,	1 50,	1 75,	1 75,	2 00,	2 00,	2 50.

Kehoe's model Clubs made to order, of any desired length or weight.

Wheelwright's Instructions in Indian Club Exercises, ten new illustrations, paper.............. 25
Kehoe's Indian Club Exercises, containing thirty illustrations from life, bound in cloth, large size, 1 00
Indian Club, Dumb bell and Sword Exercises, by Professor Harrison, illustrations, in boards 25

Fig. 2.

Fig. 1.

FOLK'S ADJUSTABLE WEIGHT INDIAN CLUB.

Patented March, 12, 1878, and Patent allowed May, 16, 1882, seven pair in one. 4, 5, 6, 7, 8, 9, and 10 lbs.

Fig. 1. is a representation in perspective of the club proper, with its three accompanying weights and detached chamberhead, said head being provided with a rubber plate on the inner side to afford a uniform bearing for the weights.

Fig. 2. is a longitudinal section showing the internal arrangement with the chamber-head attached.

This club is the same externally as the ordinary article, but is chambered in the larger end for the reception of detachable cylindrical weights which are readily, firmly, and noiselessly secured, singly or combined, in sockets in the inner end of the chamber, by a threaded metallic head.

It embraces all the sizes used by ladies, gents, misses, and youths, and is adapted to increasing strength, various movements, and different persons, being equivalent to seven pair of single weight clubs.

It is carefully turned out of the best maple, and finely polished. The weights are made of cast iron, and coppered. The other fittings are neatly set and dressed.

Club swinging is a well tried and established institution and is universally recognized as one of the best methods for developing the muscles of the body, improving the circulation, digestion, etc.

This Club with its many advantages must add greatly to the popularity of this beneficial exercise, and fully merits the favor with which it is being received. Price $5.00 per pair.

PUBLISHER'S INTRODUCTION.

As a means of physical culture, the Indian Clubs stand pre-eminent among the varied apparatus of Gymnastics now in use. Their first introduction into this country dates but a few years back, at which time very little was known of the exercise, or its origin, other than the fact that it was practiced by several celebrated English athletes, who had attained immense strength and physical development thereby. As the name implies, the Indian Club is an institution of India. In sketches of Indian life, by missionaries and travelers, we have accounts of the various national sports and pastimes of the natives, in which mention is made of the swinging of heavy war clubs, of wood, in various graceful and fantastic motions; that the performers of this exercise exhibited great muscular development and herculean strength.

Officers connected with the British Army in India also give accounts of these Indian recreations. The exercises are thus described by one of them: "The wonderful Club exercise is one of the most effectual kinds of athletic training, known anywhere in common use throughout India. The Clubs are of wood, varying in weight according to the strength of the person using them, and in length about two feet and a half, and some six or seven inches in diameter at the base, which is level, so as to admit of their standing firmly when placed on the ground, and thus affording great convenience for using them in the swinging positions.

"The exercise is in great repute among the native soldiery, police, and others whose caste renders them liable to emergencies where great strength of muscle is desirable. The evolutions which the Clubs are made to perform, in the hands of one accustomed to their use, are exceedingly graceful, and they vary almost without limit. Beside the great recommendation of simplicity, the Indian Club practice possesses the essential property of expanding the chest and exercising every muscle in the body concurrently."

Shortly after the establishment of English colonies in India, the Club exercise was introduced into the British Army as a part of the drill. The full exercise, however, according to the Indian practice, was not adopted, but a Calisthenic exercise with light Clubs was arranged, combining a few of the old Swedish Cure extension movements, more calculated to open the chest, supple the figure, and give freedom to the muscles, than to develop strength or impart practical benefit greater than might be attained by numerous other light Gymnastics, then extant. The portion adopted by the British Army may be found in "Walker's Manly Exercises," as well as a few examples from the Indian practice, vaguely and unsatisfactorily explained.

Previous to the introduction of Indian Clubs into the United States, Mr. Kehoe was extensively engaged in the manufacture and sale of Gymnastic apparatus. This well-known missionary of physical culture, having done much toward the conversion of the people of the United States to the advantages of muscular development, to enjoy a resting-spell from the cares and fatigues of business made a visit to Europe in June, 1861, returning in September of the same year. During his stay abroad he visited all the principal cities of England and Ireland, and thoroughly posted himself with everything pertaining to manly sports and exercises among the English athletes.

On the occasion of seeing Prof. Harrison, of London—a well-known English Professor of Gymnastics—use the mammoth war-clubs, he thought there must be something in it, and determined upon introducing it into the United States upon his return home. Prof. Harrison was then considered the strongest man in England, and the Queen was so pleased with his extraordinary skill in the use of these Clubs, that she presented him with an elegant vase.

On Mr. Kehoe's return to the United States he collected together his ideas, and, with his ingenuity and experience, devised a model Club, far superior to those used by Harrison, both in an ornamental and useful point of view. The present is his fourth year in their manufacture and sale, and his success in introducing them has been encouraging. With a liberal outlay and judicious management, he has built up a business which is hardly yet matured, and in course of time will have its agencies in every city and town in the country.

It would be utterly impossible to enumerate the names of well-known celebrities in manly sports who use Mr. Kehoe's Clubs, or to give a hundredth part of the testimony borne, as to the advantages they have derived from the use of them. Among the oarsmen are the names of Hammill, the Champion, Josh. Ward, the ex-Champion, and the Ward brothers; also the celebrated crews of Harvard and Yale, the Atlantics, of New York, and other celebrated clubs and oarsmen throughout the United States and the Canadas, too numerous to mention. The headquarters of the celebrated Base-Ball Clubs—the Champion Atlantics, of Brooklyn, N. Y., Mutuals, of New York, and Athletics, of Philadelphia—are all adorned with Kehoe's missives of Muscular Christianity.

In the billiard community the Clubs are esteemed invaluable, as the exercise promotes that steadiness of nerve and action required to achieve success, as well as to withstand the fatigue attending the playing of protracted games and matches. Among the noted players who are experts with the Club and Cue are Kavanagh, the ex-Champion, McDevitt, Goldthwait, Foster, Roberts, Champion of England, and a host of other Knights of the Cue, who take the lead in the beautiful and scientific game.

In the severe training undergone by those who engage in pugilistic encounters, the Club is an indispensable adjunct, and more real benefit is derived from it than from any known exercise. John C. Heenan was among the first—if not the first—to adopt it in his training in England, previous to his conflict with King. How he appreciated the exercise and its effects, in a moral and physical point of view, may be learned from the following letter from Mr. Heenan to Mr. Kehoe.

9

NEWMARKET, ENGLAND, Nov. 12, 1863.

S. D. KEHOE:

DEAR SIR :—The Indian Clubs which you so kindly sent on from New York, for me to use during my training, have been forwarded from London by Owen Swift, and although scarcely a week has elapsed since I have commenced using them, their beneficial results are the subject of much commendation from my trainer, Jack McDonald, and my friends and backers. As an assistant for training purposes, and imparting strength to the muscles of the arms, wrists, and hands, together, in fact, with the whole muscular system, I do not know of their equal , and I find by experience that the popularity in which your Clubs are held by Professors of Gymnastics in various parts of my native country, is fully deserved, and at no distant day they will become one of the institutions of America. At this particular time they will prove of immense advantage, and I cannot but thank you for the unsolicited interest you take in my welfare and success. These Clubs need no recommendation at my hands, and I have only to tender my heartiest wishes for your prosperity and success. With many thanks for your kindness, I remain,

Yours truly,   JOHN C. HEENAN.

Nor are the beneficial effects of the Club exercise by any means confined to professionals of the various manly sports and pastimes. Merchants, bankers, clerks, and those engaged in daily business pursuits, who need some available means of exercise to counteract the ills arising from their sedentary occupations, are many of them becoming experts with the Clubs, and reaping everlasting benefits. Note in the crowded thoroughfare of Broadway now and then an occasional passer-by, with well-knit and shapely form, firm and elastic step, broad-chested and full-blooded, and you may mark him down as one of Kehoe's converts. The names of these well-known New Yorkers are too numerous for mention here.

Mr. Kehoe's determination to make the Indian Club an American institution has been rewarded by a success beyond his most sanguine expectations. A single glance at his order book exhibits the names of our most distinguished generals, statesmen, lawyers, and divines, whom he has supplied with his anti-dyspeptic, anti-consumptive, and anti to every ill that flesh is heir to, promoters of physical strength and symmetrical form. Among the host of distinguished personages above referred to are found the names of Gen. Grant and his entire staff; Hon. R. E. Fenton, Governor of New York, and staff; Hon. Schuyler Colfax, and so on through the Army and Navy, Cabinet and Congress, Pulpit and Bar.

The following letter explains itself:

HEADQUARTERS ARMIES OF THE UNITED STATES,
Washington, D. C., April 9, 1866.

MR. S. D. KEHOE, 103 ELM ST., NEW YORK:

DEAR SIR :—I have the pleasure of acknowledging the receipt of a full set of rosewood Dumb-Bells and Indian Clubs, of your manufacture. They are of the nicest workmanship.

Please accept my thanks for your thus remembering me, and particularly my boys, who I know will take great delight as well as receive benefit in using them.

Yours truly.   U. S. GRANT, Lieut.-Gen. U. S. A.

Mr. Kehoe has long felt the necessity of a manual of instruction in the Club exercises. There are many who have purchased Clubs, who have no time, or, perhaps, opportunity, to attend a Gymnasium, and thus have no means of learning the beauties of the exercise as performed by experts, which are only to be attained by instruction and practice. Confined, therefore, to a few simple movements of their own invention, calculated, perhaps, to do as much harm as good, as well as being devoid of anything attractive or pleasing, they soon tire of the Clubs, and throw them by with disgust.

The fact is, that but very few of the Gymnasiums throughout the country have arranged or introduced the exercise with anything like system, nor do they seem to be acquainted with the manifold graceful and artistic evolutions that have of late years been remodeled and extended from the Indian practice. The author trusts that the manual may meet the requirements of those for whom it is intended, and that they may reap the full advantage of the benefits and beauties of the exercise

GENERAL REMARKS ON PHYSICAL CULTURE.

EDUCATION is divided into two branches—Physical and Moral. More correctly might it be divided into three—Physical, Moral, and Intellectual. Nothing is more certain than that the intellectual and the moral powers may be educated separately; the former being amended while the latter are not, and the converse. Facts in proof of this are abundant. There is as real a distinction between moral and intellectual education, as there is between physical education and either of them. Moral action, intellectual action, and physical action, have their seats and instruments in different parts of the human system; and those parts are essentially connected by sympathy, as well as other ties more mechanical and obvious, and they are all three so intimately connected, that the improvement of any one of them may be made to contribute to that of the others. One of them being injured or benefited, therefore, the others are affected in a corresponding manner. Deriving their being and sustenance from the same source, and serving as elements of the same individual person, each of whose parts is necessary to the integrity and perfection of the whole, it would be singular were it not so.

The organized system of man constitutes the machinery with which alone his mind operates during their connection as soul and body. Improve the apparatus, then, and you facilitate and improve the work which the mind performs with it, precisely as you facilitate steam operation, and enhance its product, by improving the machinery with which it is executed. In one case, steam, and in the other, spirit, continue unchanged; and each works and produces with a degree of perfection corresponding to that of the instrument it employs.

Hence physical education is far more important than is commonly imagined. Without a due regard to it, and a stricter and more judicious attention than is paid to it at present, man cannot attain the perfection of his nature. Ancient Greece might be cited in confirmation of this. If history and other forms of record be credited, the people of that country were, as a nation, physically and intellectually, the most perfect of the human race; and there is every reason to believe that their unrivaled attention to physical culture was influential in producing the result.

As mankind act from motives of necessity and interest, much more than from those of any other sort, physical education, the chief source of superior strength of person, has been greatly neglected, especially by the higher orders of society, for two or three centuries. Knowledge being now the only ground of power and influence, intellectual education receives at present a much more exclusive attention than it formerly did, and much more than comports with the benefit of our race.

The cultivation of bodily strength, in preference to everything else, would establish only the right of the strongest, as it is found to exist in the origin of society. To cultivate the faculties of the mind exclusively, would produce only the weakness of sentiment or excess of passion. There is, for every individual, a means of making all these dispositions act in harmony · and the due blending of physical and moral education alone can produce it. Let it be remembered that young persons will much more easily be withdrawn from the application they ought to pay to the study of the sciences, by insipid recreations and trifling games, than by the fatiguing exercises necessary for their development and the preservation of their health, which, however, habit soon renders easy and delightful.

An examination of the human frame demonstrates that it was intended for motion alternately with repose, and not for a state of absolute quiescence. Nor is the mind, which is furnished with so many faculties, and provided with so many organs of sense, which serve to connect it with the external world, less calculated for active exertion. Any attempt to contravene the laws of nature, which enjoin a reasonable exercise of mind and body, brings a punishment upon the individual. The mind, which he allows to be inactive, loses the capacity for exertion when required, and the body becomes a prey to disease in some shape or form. Let it never be forgotten, however, that the physical education of the human race ought not to be alone confined to the humble object of preventing disease. Its aim should be loftier and more in accordance with the destiny and character of its subject—to raise man to the summit of his nature; and such will be its scope in future and more enlightened times.

The general utility of exercise, then, will only be questioned by those who are not aware that the health and vigor of all the bodily organs depend on the proportioned exercise of each. In active exertion, the member exercised swells with the more frequent and copious flow of blood, and greater abundance of heat is developed in it; and if we repeat the same motions many times, after intervals of repose, all the muscles exercised become permanently developed; a perfection of action ensues in the member exercised, which it d'd not previously possess, any deformity by which it is affected is corrected, and strength and activity are acquired. That man, therefore, gains the most strength, who engages in muscular exercises that require the application of much power, but which are sufficiently separated by intervals of repose.

The nature of the muscular fiber need not be discussed here; it is enough for us to remark, that, to execute its functions properly, it must be in a certain state of tension, that it may be possessed of sufficient elasticity. A cord proceeding from a fixed point cannot influence a movable body till it be drawn tight; so a muscle cannot raise a limb unless it possesses a certain degree of tightness.

The difference in the power of muscles varies greatly, according to the state of health, or disease, of the individual. If a muscle be taken from an animal in good health, it will not only bear a greater weight than the same muscle taken from an animal which has long been sick, but the former will be many days going into decay, allowing the weight to drop, while the latter will decay very speedily. To maintain the muscular fibers in the first condition, a due supply of blood and nervous energy is requisite.

The great bulk of the human body is composed of muscle. If you look at the bare skeleton, composed chiefly of hollow bones, you will see how slender an outline of the human form it presents. The clothing of those bones, the closing of the cavities, the formation of the special human outline, is the work of the muscles; the weight of the individual depends chiefly on them.

If we could lay aside the protecting layer of skin and fat which envelopes the body, it would make very little difference in its size, and we should then see the muscular body, red and well defined, and realize more fully how very large a proportion of the body is formed by muscle. It is, as known in the flesh of animals, the lean meat. Its structure is regular and beautiful; we can form no idea of this structure from the meat which we cut at the table, because we generally cut across the grain. If we cut an orange in two, transversely, we can form little idea of its structure; but if we peel it, and split it longitudinally, we then see at a glance the number of parts which compose it, the semi-transparent membrane which incloses each division, the way in which they are united; then if we open one of these divisions we find inside the seed, and the juicy pulp; and even the pulp, now, will present quite a different aspect from the transverse section, for we see that it is arranged in little bundles or fibers lying side by side, and that each bundle is itself incased in such a delicate transparent membrane, that it tears and lets out the juice with every attempt to separate it. Thus, by carefully dissecting the orange, we get a totally different idea of its structure, than by simply cutting it through.

Now, in the same way, if we could peel the human being of its skin rind, we should find the muscles below as well marked as the sections of the orange; each muscle carefully enveloped in its sheath of membrane, and lying across or beside other muscles similarly enveloped. The number amounts to several hundred, spread all over the body, infinitely varied in shape and size. Some are so large they almost cover the trunk, others so small as to be almost invisible. They are thick and short, long and slender, according to the view and object to be attained, and the part where it is to be attained.

Muscles are mostly in pairs; and the layers which cover the right arm, correspond to those which cover the left. So with those on the legs, and those which cover the face, neck, and chest. They are symmetrical throughout the body, most beautifully so, and the line of beauty is illustrated so perfectly in no part of the body, as in the muscles. This whole assemblage of muscles, so varied, and spreading over the entire body, is the muscular system. Its grand object is movement.

The principle on which exercise acts is evident, the immediate effect being an increase, both in the size and power of the muscles exercised, in consequence of an admirable law which obtains in living bodies, that (within certain limits) in proportion to the exertion which it is required to make, a part increases not only in strength and fitness, but also in size.

Instances of the application of this law may be seen daily, by noting the effect produced on a person who takes regular special exercise. Not only is he improved in strength and dexterity, but the muscles, brought into unusual action, increase rapidly in size and vigor, so as soon to surpass those of the rest of the body which have been less employed. Nor does the beneficial influence stop here. If the exercise be not carried so far as to produce excessive fatigue, all other parts of the body sympathize with the improving condition of that which is chiefly exerted; the circulation excited from time to time by the exercise acquires new vigor, and the blood being thrown with unusual force into all parts of the system, all the functions are carried on with increased activity, an improvement in the general health is soon manifested, and the mind (if at the same time judiciously cultivated) acquires strength, and is rendered more capable of prolonged exertion.

Having discoursed at some length on the important benefits to be derived from physical culture, and the direct action of exercise on the muscular system, whereby these benefits are imparted, we will now describe some of the special means of exercise common in this country, and the particular advantages of the Indian Club practice, of which this work alone treats.

Of the various species of exercise, that of walking is the most common, for obvious reasons. The majority of the American people, however, derive its benefits from force of necessity, as but a small proportion of them do any more of it than they are obliged to. Notice the cars and omnibuses of our metropolis—the majority of the occupants being persons of sedentary employments, suffering in bodily health for want of sufficient exercise; cooped up all day at the counting-house, and then jammed into the crowded stage or street car, to breathe an air worse than the black hole of Calcutta. They sit down to dinner—is it a wonder they take to the "bitter" resort for an appetite, and the "morning call" to relieve the pangs of dyspepsia?

Others are more judicious. Instead of bitters, they prefer walking, which they find in the end a cheaper and more effectual appetizer, with a consequent healthful nutrition.

But walking is not a sufficient or proper amount of exercise, for persons of sedentary occupations. Many finding this to be the case, and having no time or means at hand to adopt any other, resort to an undue amount of pedestrianism. In the end they find that this does not produce the results anticipated, that they gain no increase of muscular power in the chest and arms, and no development of these parts, so essential to a graceful form and figure. In fact, instances are of common occurrence, where the exercise of walking has been carried to such an extent as to produce unproportionate development between the upper and lower extremities, owing to the well-known physiological fact that any undue exercise of particular muscles, only weakens the others.

To those accustomed to Gymnasiums and gymnastic exercises, the truth of this is clearly demonstrated by examples of disproportionate development of various kinds. In a complete Gymnasium there is found a variety of gymnastic apparatus, too numerous to specify here, constructed with reference to the training of the entire muscular system. The Gymnast, in his routine of exercise, after having fatigued one set of muscles, changes the apparatus to employ another set, and so on through the various evolutions on poles, bars, ladders, rings, &c., uniformly exerting his muscular system, with the object of giving each particular part or member its proportional development. This is the proper method of exercise, though there are many to be found, in the gymnastic classes of every Gymnasium, who become devoted to some special exercise, or particular feat, requiring the distorted development of some particular set of muscles, to the detriment of the rest. Thus it is common to see disproportioned forms, in persons with arms that, in comparison with the rest of the figure, would suffice for legs, and legs disproportioned to the upper extremities.

The majority of newly enlisted members of our public Gymnasiums are young men, to whom exercise has been prescribed by some physician, as a medicine. It is a noticeable fact that nearly all of them are at first disproportionately developed, relatively between the upper and lower extremities, the latter in nearly every case preponderant. This is easily accounted for from the fact that walking has been their only exercise. In a short time, however, the influence of the parallel bars, Indian Clubs, and dumb bells begins to show itself in the expansion of the chest, swelling of the muscles on the arms, breast, and loins, to their proper and natural development. The pads of the tailor are no longer needed, and the shoulders are squared with sinews and muscle, instead of the artificial inventions of the "ninth part of a man."

We have other means of exercise than the Gymnasium, in our various national sports, such as base ball, boating, and other manly pastimes; but these do not come within the reach of all. Men of business, or their clerks and employes, have no time to devote to such amusements, and even if they do take a few days, in the course of a year, to pull an oar or play a game of ball, the result is invariably a strain of the back, sprain of the ankle, twist of the wrist, or some other mishap, and a week or more following, of pain and misery.

The fact of the case is, the American people seem to have no time to exercise, even if they had the means at hand. The Gymnasium is always come-at-able, in most of our large cities, but the time cannot be spared to attend it. Thus physical culture is neglected, for want of time, as eating would be, did not the Almighty wisely provide for man's negligence, by warning him with hunger, that he had neglected something. So has he provided for a warning and punishment to those who are neglecting their physical condition, which will come sooner or later.

It has before been stated, that as a means of physical culture, the Indian Club stands pre-eminent among the varied apparatus of gymnastics now in use. This fact is unquestionable, as those who know how to use them are ready to attest. For simplicity and convenience, they are unsurpassed by any other kind of apparatus, and half the fixtures of an ordinary Gymnasium will not produce such a general development of the muscles from the loins upwards, as a pair of Clubs.

To those, then, who say they have no time for exercise, we heartily recommend the Indian Clubs, which, in connection with a daily walk of a few miles, will be just exactly what is required to secure physical perfection and muscular strength, without putting yourself to but very little trouble to attain it. A half hour with the Clubs, daily, morning and evening, or to suit convenience it need not be so divided, but may all be taken in the morning, or all in the evening, will, in connection with walking, keep the muscular system in perfect condition, and thus insure perfect bodily health. To those who aspire to more than ordinary development and strength, take more than ordinary exercise with the Clubs, and you can attain what you desire, to almost any limit.

Exercise should never be taken immediately after a plentiful meal, nor should it be taken to excess, particularly during hot weather. In the former case too much cerebral influence for the time being expended in muscular action, the amount of it conveyed to the stomach is insufficient for the laborious function that viscus has to perform, and indigestion is the consequence. It is possible to fatigue the body beyond a proper point, in which case repose becomes necessary; but this is a rare occurrence compared with the instances of insufficient exercise, or where the mind is stretched beyond its natural power to bear, by the ambitious student, the covetous and care-worn merchant, or the adventurer in political life.

Where older people have neglected exercise it is more difficult to induce them to resume its use, but some such device as the following may be tried. "Ogul, a voluptuary who could be managed but with difficulty by his physician, on finding himself extremely ill from indulgence and intemperance, requested advice. 'Eat a basilisk stewed in rose water,' replied the physician. In vain did the slaves search for a basilisk until they met with Zadig, who, approaching Ogul, exclaimed, 'Behold that which thou desirest! But, my lord,' continued he, 'it is not to be eaten; all its virtues must enter through thy pores. I have therefore inclosed it in a little ball, blown up, and covered with a fine skin. Thou must strike the ball with all thy might, and I must strike it back again, for a considerable time, and by observing this regimen, and taking no other drink than rose water for a few days, thou wilt see and acknowledge the effects of my art.'

"The first day Ogul was out of breath, and thought he should have died of fatigue. The second he was less fatigued, and slept better. In eight days he recovered all his strength. Zadig then said to him, 'There is no such

:hing in nature as a basilisk! but thou hast taken exercise, and been temperate, and hast therefore recovered thy health.' "

The Indian Clubs will be found as useful for those confined by the weather within doors during the winter months, as the ball of Zadig.

By no means of exercise has such remarkable development of muscle and strength been attained in such a short space of time, as by the Indian Club practice. We will cite a few examples of this fact, and present portraitures of several celebrated athletes of New York City, who owe their immense physical power chiefly to the Club exercise.

Our first portrait is that of Mr. J. Edward Russell, a well-known amateur Gymnast of New York.

Mr. Russell was born in the city, and at quite an early age showed a fondness for manly sports. When but a youth he was celebrated as an expert swimmer, and attracted crowds to the Battery baths, to witness his performances in swimming. When but fifteen years of age he became a member of the well-known Crosby Street Gymnasium, founded by Professor Ottignon, from which institution nearly all the noted Gymnasts of this country are graduates. Young Russell made remarkable progress in the various gymnastic exercises, and was particularly fond of the "Art of Self-Defense," making very rapid progress in sparring, under the tuition of the renowned Ottignon, and was his favorite pupil.

After the old Crosby Street Gymnasium passed into other hands, and the well-known and elegant Gymnasium of Professor John Wood was erected on Twenty-eighth Street and Fifth Avenue, Mr. Russell joined the classes of the latter, where he has ever since been enrolled as a member. For the past few years, being still quite a young man, he has been actively identified with our principal base-ball and boat clubs, and is always on hand when any hard work is to be done.

J. EDWARD RUSSELL.

Mr. Russell's favorite exercise is the Indian Clubs, in which he excels, having won the Champion Medal, at the great Gymnastic Tourney, at Irving Hall, on the first of May, 1866, presented to the best performer with the Indian Clubs, by Mr. Kehoe. The Club exercise was the principal feature of the evening's entertainments, and several celebrated experts with the Clubs competed for the medal and the championship. The decision of the judges was unanimously in favor of Mr. Russell, and to him was awarded the medal, which is an elegant affair, of which the holder may justly be proud. It is of solid gold, and the work of Tiffany & Co., of New York. The following engraving is a fac-simile of it.

Medal presented to Mr. J. Edward Russell—winner of the Club Tourney, at Irving Hall, May 1, 1866, and Champion of America—by S. D. Kehoe.

Mr. Russell is a gentleman much respected by all who know him, and is engaged in mercantile pursuits. Though an ardent admirer of, and adept in, all the manly sports, he is in no way classed as a professional. On several occasions he has refused tempting offers to enter into professional engagements, preferring the uncertainties of Wall Street.

Our next portrait will be recognized by all who have ever seen the good-natured and jovial face of Mr. Timothy Dermody, the well-known Professor of the Club exercise.

Mr. Dermody has attained a physical development rarely equaled, from a constant practice with the Clubs during the past four or five years. He has also been instrumental in introducing the beauties of the exercise to a great extent in New York City, and has always been found ready and willing to impart information on the subject. The Professor has a few movements of his own arrangement, that are particularly difficult, and require almost superhuman strength in their execution. In many of the exercises he has no equal.

Mr. Dermody is in the prime of life—a fine specimen of muscular activity, and one of the first and foremost in our manly recreations. In point of physical development he has attained rare perfection. His muscular system exhibits a general development of a high order, and though not in complete training, his appearance would indicate that he was.

Like Mr. Russell, Mr. Dermody is also engaged in business pursuits, at present merchandising in Brooklyn. Though we have styled him "Professor," he does not make the manly sports a profession, but only a pastime, and his instructions in the Club exercise have always been imparted gratis.

The Club exercise, as practiced by Mr. Russell and Mr. Dermody, differ somewhat in style, the former being particularly proficient in the entire practice, and all the difficult movements, with Clubs of medium weight, while the latter executes several very difficult movements, peculiar to himself, with Clubs of heavy weight. We may take occasion here to remark, that there are personages of Club notoriety, who, by falsely representing the weight of the Clubs they use, have led the public to understand that it is a common thing to use Clubs weighing from thirty to fifty pounds each. A pair of Clubs weighing thirty pounds each is rarely used, and there are but one or two men in this country who can perform more than a few simple movements with thirty pound Clubs.

TIMOTHY DERMODY.

If any one thinks he can refute this statement, and has seen performances where greater weights have been used, let him, on the next occasion, weigh the Clubs himself, instead of taking the figures for granted, that may be given or marked on them.

It is a general failing—if it may be called a failing—for the athlete to be proud of his strength, and to be in no wise backward in exhibiting it at every favorable opportunity. This is all right and proper, provided no deception is used, which, we are sorry to say, is too often the case, and the conscience, with the weight of the Club and dumb bells, is easily stretched. Scripture says, "The glory of a young man is his strength;" but it also says, "A false balance is an abomination to the Lord, but a just weight is his delight."

Perhaps no institution on the face of the globe has turned out any better Gymnasts or stronger men than the Olympic Club of San Francisco, California; yet they lay no claim to such remarkable performances as we see recorded daily, in reports of gymnastic exhibitions and athletic entertainments, in other States. At a recent exhibition, given by the members of this Club, Mr. Charles Bennett, who is termed the "young California Hercules," used twenty pound Clubs in a variety of movements, and held fifty-two pounds in each hand, at arm's length, with ease. These are both excellent feats of strength, and would puzzle many of our thirty pound Club swingers, and heavy dumb bell men.

Mr. Charles A. Quitzow, the subject of our next sketch, is a well-known amateur Gymnast, of Brooklyn. Mr. Quitzow, and Mr. Avon C. Burnham, the proprietor of the new Brooklyn Gymnasium, are among the pioneers of Gymnasts in that city, and were brother athletes some fifteen years ago. Those who may have attended the old Brooklyn Gymnasium will recollect the excellent double posturing act performed by them.

Mr. Quitzow has always been passionately fond of gymnastics, and excelled as a Gymnast. He was among the first in adopting the Indian Club practice, and although for the past four or five years he has neglected the Gymnasium, he retains remarkable strength, and handles a pair of thirty pound Clubs with ease. Mr. Quitzow is a New York merchant, and his physique bears testimony to the benefits derived from exercise, and the magic effects of using the Indian Clubs.

Our last sketch will be that of Mr. Fred. Küner, a young New York artist. Though but twenty-two years of age, he has attained a development of remarkable perfection, exclusively with the Indian Clubs, he rarely taking any other exercise. Mr. Küner is an example of proportional development, and is a model of manly form. Many New Yorkers will remember the celebrated statue of the Indian Hunter, lately on exhibition on Broadway. The artist of this beautiful work of art was indebted to the kindness of Mr. Küner, who served as a model, in the study of the anatomy of the figure, which is, perhaps, the finest piece of anatomical modeling ever executed in this country.

To those who are skeptical regarding the efficiency of the Clubs as a means of exercise, independent of other means, we would refer to Mr. Küner, as to what results may be attained by proper and regular practice.

CHARLES A. QUITZOW

FREDERICK KÜNER

INTRODUCTORY TO THE EXERCISES.

DESCRIPTION OF THE CLUB.

The Indian Club exercise, as practiced at the present day in the different Gymnasiums and institutions of physical training throughout the country, is properly divided into two distinct kinds: one with the short and light Club, or Bat, and the other with the long Club, or Indian Club proper. The author does not deem it necessary to introduce the exercises for the light Club in this work, as they are only adapted for invalids and children. To those who need them we would refer to a work on "Light Gymnastics," by Dr. Dio Lewis, of Boston, Mass.

It will therefore be understood, that the exercises in this work are exclusively for the long Clubs. They are used in pairs, and vary in length from twenty-four to twenty-eight inches, and in weight, commonly, from four to twenty pounds each, or from eight to forty pounds to the pair.

The shape of the Club may be seen in any of the illustrations, but it varies somewhat, in accordance with the weight. This is necessary to give it a proper balance, and the general proportions are of particular importance, as the movements are rendered more easy and graceful than they would be if attempted with an ill-proportioned, shapeless Club.

WEIGHT FOR BEGINNERS.

The proper weight for beginners depends, of course, upon condition and strength, but can be approximately arrived at as follows· As a general rule, the proper weight may be determined by holding a pair horizontally at the side, at arm's length, letting them down to a perpendicular, and raising them again, several times, grasping them at the extremity of the handles. If this cannot be done after several trials, the Club is too heavy, and a lighter pair must be tried, until you obtain a fit.

The majority of beginners, and even somewhat advanced Gymnasts—if they have never used the Club—will find that from six to ten pounds is sufficient weight to start with. It is almost a universal mistake in trying to use Clubs that are too heavy. It must be understood that it is not sufficient to be able to execute a few simple evolutions with a Club, and then consider yourself a graduate; for the real benefit can only be derived from a protracted exercise of difficult movements and artistic combinations, calculated to bring into play every known muscle—and to discover many unknown ones—from the loins upwards.

It is therefore recommended that the novice commence with a weight that he can easily manage, and with which he can execute the preliminary exercises. As he progresses, the weight may be increased, in proportion as the strength develops.

HOLDING THE CLUB.

It is a very important matter to learn to hold the Club properly, as a careless or negligent manner of grasping the handle will prevent the attainment of a graceful style of swinging, as well as endanger some bystander's head.

Take good care to grasp the handle firmly, close to the ball, extending the thumb along the shank, which you will find enables you to control its movement, and prevent it from wandering out of the direction you desire it to go. This is the general hold, where the thumb can be used to guide the movements.

In the Moulinéts—a bent arm and wrist movement—it will hereafter be shown that it is necessary to relax the grasp, holding the Club entirely between the thumb and forefinger during a part of the movement, but regaining a complete hold again on the finish.

POSITION

Before entering into the details of the exercises, it is of the utmost importance to attend to what is termed position.

The first question of importance on this subject is, What position of the feet affords the greatest solidity in standing? It is not necessary to enter into a detail of the numerous controversies by which some have defended or repudiated the position with the toes turned outward: it will be sufficient to state the fact, that the larger the base of support, the firmer and more solid will the position be, and to adopt as a fundamental one, the military position, which has been found practically the best, by those who have nothing else to do but to walk.

The equal squareness of the body and shoulders to the front is the first great principle of position. The heels must be in a line, and closed; the knees straight; the toes turned out, with the feet forming an angle of sixty degrees; the arms hanging close to the body; the elbows turned in, and close to the sides; the body upright, but inclining forward, so that the weight of it may bear principally upon the balls of the feet; the head erect, and eyes straight to the front.

There are two positions of the Clubs which we will now proceed to describe, which are the starting-points of the various movements in the exercises.

THE FIRST POSITION.

With a Club in each hand, grasping the handle according to the foregoing instructions, assume the military position, with the Clubs hanging pendant at the side. (See Figure 5.) This is the first position.

THE SECOND POSITION.

From the first position, raise both Clubs to a perpendicular, holding them directly in front of the body, the hands the height of and opposite to the shoulder, and about six inches in front. Hold both Clubs exactly parallel and perpendicular. (See position of left Club, Figure 13.) This is the second position

These two positions will often be referred to in the following explanations.

CONCLUSION.

Before commencing with the exercises, it only remains for us to refer to the time and circumstances of exercise, as has been previously directed in the "General Remarks on Physical Culture," remembering that your progress will depend on the observance of those rules. A belt, or cincture, is of utility, and though not absolutely required, it would be well to be provided with one.

THE ALPHABET OF THE CLUB EXERCISE.

To readily comprehend and execute the different movements described
in the exercises, it will be necessary to commence at first principles, and learn
the Alphabet of Clubs—which consists of eight different movements, to be
executed with the right or left hand, with a single Club. The various figures,
and apparently difficult and complicated movements, that are executed by
experts in Club swinging, are only combinations of these eight motions, which
may be transformed and arranged, producing an endless variety of beautiful
and graceful exercises.

THE ALPHABET.

The following are the eight distinct movements of the Alphabet:

1st. INNER FRONT CIRCLE.	5th. INNER SIDE CIRCLE.
2d. OUTER FRONT CIRCLE.	6th. OUTER SIDE CIRCLE.
3d. INNER BACK CIRCLE.	7th. INNER MOULINET.
4th. OUTER BACK CIRCLE.	8th. OUTER MOULINET.

Two of these movements—the first and second—are executed in front
of the body; two—the third and fourth—back of the body; and the remain-
ing four at the side.

Strictly classing the movements of the Alphabet, there are but four totally
different; for the only difference between outer and inner circles is simply a
reverse of the direction of the sweep.

We will now proceed to describe them separately.

THE INNER FRONT CIRCLE.

With a Club in each hand, assume the first position. (See Figure 5.)

Toe a line or crack in the floor, as a guide for direction, and reference for the explanations.

Carry the right hand Club to the left, in a direction parallel to the floor line, and describe complete sweeps or circles in front of the body, at arm's length.

Repeat successively several times.

Execute the same movement with the left hand, carrying the Club toward the right. Though in this case the direction is reversed, it is nevertheless an Inner Front Circle

THE OUTER FRONT CIRCLE.

From the first position, carry the right hand Club outwardly to the right, and in a direction parallel to the floor line, describe the Outer Front Circle, which is simply a reverse of the Inner Front.

Execute the Outer Front with the left hand, carrying the Club outwardly to the left, and describing a reverse sweep from that of the Inner Front, with the left hand.

Repeat these movements separately, and perfectly familiarize yourself with the distinction between the Outer and Inner Front Circles.

THE INNER BACK CIRCLE.

We now come to a movement of a different character. Instead of a sweep in front of the body, with arms at full length, the Back Circles are described behind the body, with the arms bent.

Assume the second position, raising the Clubs perpendicularly in front of the body, with the hands the height of, and six inches in front of, the shoulders. The position for both hands will be the same as that given for the left hand in Figure 13.

Commence the movement by carrying the Club in the right hand upward and backward, to the left, over the head, (to position shown in Figure 12,) and in the same movement letting it drop downward, describing a circle. The hand will remain just behind the shoulder, and its position but little changed in the movement.

Execute the same with the left hand, starting the movement as shown in Figure 12, by the dotted arm and Club, B.

Endeavor to swing the Club squarely, and let the evolutions be perpendicular, and parallel to the floor line.

THE OUTER BACK CIRCLE.

The only difference between this movement and the Inner Back, is that the direction is reversed, and instead of dropping the Club inwardly, from the positions shown in Figure 12, it is carried outwardly, in the direction shown by the dotted Club, Figure 13.

From the second position, carry the Club in the right hand to the position above referred to, (Figure 13,) and let it fall outward and downward, in the direction A, describing a circle just the reverse of the Inner Back.

Execute the Outer Back with the left hand—the position of which, at the commencement of the movement, may be seen in Figure 14—letting the Club drop in the direction A.

THE INNER SIDE CIRCLE.

Assume the first position.

The Side Circles are to be described at the sides of the body, and directly across and at right angles with the floor line.

Carry the Club in the right hand directly backward, and at arm's length describe a complete circle at the side, and crossing the floor line.

Favor the movement by turning the body slightly as the Club goes backward, and endeavor to execute the circle fairly and squarely.

With the left hand repeat the same movement, in the same manner.

THE OUTER SIDE CIRCLE.

Reverse the preceding movement.

From the first position, carry the Club in the right hand forward and outward, and complete the circle.

Execute the movement with the left hand.

THE INNER MOULINET.

This movement is properly a side circle, but is executed with the bent arm, instead of full length sweeps. It is called the Moulinet, from its being like a movement in the broadsword exercise, so named.

With a Club in each hand, assume the second position.

Now let the Club in the right hand fall directly forward and outward from the body, at the same time relaxing the grasp, and allowing it to turn freely between the thumb and torefinger, as it passes to the side and backward. Thu. describe a side circle, with as little movement of the arm as possible, doing most of the work with the wrist.

Execute this movement with the left hand.

THE OUTER MOULINET.

This is a reverse of the Inner Moulinet, and will require some little practice to execute smoothly.

From the second position, let the Club in the right hand fall backward, and by a twist of the wrist carry it entirely around, in a direction the reverse of the Inner Moulinet.

Try the same with the left hand.

After having become familiar with the foregoing eight movements, so as to execute them with some degree of correctness, you may commence the Exercises.

BOXING AND CONTEST GLOVES.

WE ARE

SOLE AGENTS

For the Sale of

BUTT'S

PATENT GLOVES

Patented September 3d, 1878

Which are used exclusively by all the prominent athletes throughout the country. These gloves are made with solid palms; the fingers are made by stitching double fourchettes inside of the glove, and with one half the stitching that is required in an old style Glove; and no stitching comes inside to touch the hand in any part, to rot out with perspiration, thus causing them to rip.

No. A.—Boys', are made of soft tan leather palms, and chamois coverings, and stuffed with curled hair. Price per set, two pair, $2 50

No. B.—Men's, made of the same as above, but better quality leather and hair. Price per set, two pair, $3 00

No. C.—Made of extra tan leather, palms and wrists bound with blue fancy leather and strings to tighten around the wrist; stuffed with curled hair, and sewed in with an extra band of leather, with double stitching to keep the hair in place. Price per set, two pair, $3 50

No. D.—Same as No. C, only heel padded... $4 00

No. E.—Are made with white kid palms with blue fancy leather cuffs, and elastic to tighten around the wrists; extra soft coverings, stuffed with curled hair, and double sewn in with an extra band of leather, with ventilated palms..$4 50

No. F.—Same as No. E, only heel padded.... .... 5 00

No. G.—Are made with soft tan dog-skin palms, with red fancy leather cuffs, and elastic to tighten around the wrists, and extra fine soft covering, stuffed with curled hair, and double sewn in with an extra band of leather, with ventilated palms...Price, per set, $5 50

No. H.—Same as No. G, only heel padded... 6 00

No. I.—Peck & Snyder's Professional Sounding Gloves are made with reindeer, Indian tanned palms: with white kid coverings, and with red, white and blue cuffs of fancy leather; stuffed with the best curled hair, and double sewn in with an extra band of leather, and with ventilated palms................Price per set, $6 50

No. P.—Same as No. I, only heel padded.... / 7 00

No. K.—Are made of imported white French kid; palms and coverings of the very best material; finished with long red, white, and blue fancy leather cuffs, nicely stitched with silk, &c., with ventilated palms.
Price per set, 7 50

No. L.—Same as No. K, only heel padded .... $ 00

No. M'.—Or the Marquis of Queensborough Professional Contest Gloves.

This Glove is made to lace up at the back under the hair in order to tighten it to any size hand, with white kid covering. The tops of the fingers are outside, so the hand can be closed as easily as in a kid glove.
Price per set, two pair, $6 00

Sample sets, by express, on receipt of price, or by registered mail, at our risk, on receipt of price and 50 cents per pair additional for postage and registering.

Boxing Made Easy ; or the complete manual of self-defense, clearly explained and illust'd. Price, 15c.

The Science of Self-Defense. By Edmund Price. 130pp. Illust'd. and bound. By mail, " 75c.

The Art of Boxing. By Ned Donnelly Professor of Boxing to the London Athletic Club. 35 double figure illustrations with others.......................................Cloth bound, 50c., paper cover, 25c.

This is the most complete work on the subject yet published.

N. B.—Owing to the great demand for a cheap kid and chamois Boxing Glove, we offer the following, which for cheapness and quality cannot be surpassed.

No. OO.—Boys, made of soft Tan Leather palms, Chamois Covering and stuffed with curled hair, a good cheap glove, price, per set, two pairs, $2.00.

No. O.—Men's, made same as No. OO, but better goods and hair, price per set, two pairs, $2.50.

No. EE.—Reindeer palms and white kid covering, stuffed with hair, price, per set, two pairs, $5.00.

No. CC.—Dog Skin palms, kid covering, stuffed with hair, cheapest kid glove made, price, per set, two pairs, $4.50.

All the above Boxing Gloves are warranted not to harden by water or perspiration.

Exercise No. 1.

This is a simple extension movement, and is easily understood by referring to the figure.

Assume the first position. Raise the Clubs slowly, crossing them in front, (see figure,) with the palms of the hands outwards.

Extend the arms outwardly, as far as possible, without changing the position of the hands, and raise the right hand Club slowly upward, to the position shown in the figure by the dotted lines.

Execute the same movement with the left hand.

Do all this slowly, noticing the position of the hands in the figure. Keep the Clubs always perpendicular.

Repeat until fatigued.

Exercise No. 2.

This is an extension movement also.

Assume the first position, then the second.

Carry the Clubs to the position shown in the figure, and then raise and lower them slowly, as shown by the dotted lines.

Keep both Clubs in a horizontal position, and parallel to the floor line.

Repeat slowly until fatigued.

A variation of this exercise may be had by endeavoring to turn the Clubs backward, so that their ends may touch, and not bring the hands any nearer together than is shown in the figure.

40

FIGURE 2.

Exercise No. 3.

Take the second position.

Carry the Clubs at arm's length to the side, holding them perpendicu larly, as shown in the figure.

Grasp the handle firmly, and fully extend the arm. Let it fall slowly, until the base touches the shoulder, describing the curve A B, in the direction indicated in the figure.

Do this with both Clubs simultaneously, and raise them slowly to a perpendicular again, keeping the arms fully extended.

In letting the Club down to the shoulder, you must relax the grasp, in order to keep the arm perfectly straight, which you will find impossible to do otherwise.

Now, from the position in the figure, let the Clubs downward slowly, to the front, in the direction indicated in the diagram, until they hang perpendicularly, as the dotted Club, C. In this movement the hold need not be relaxed.

Raise them again to the former position, and repeat the movement until fatigued.

A variation of this exercise may be had, by letting them fall backward until they hang perpendicularly, raising them to the first position again.

These movements are particularly beneficial in strengthening the wrist, and will assist you materially in executing the Moulinets.

42

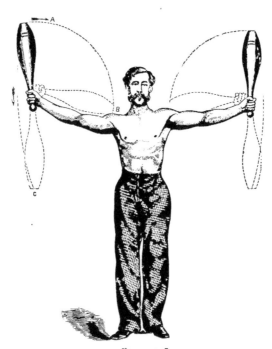

FIGURE 3

Exercise No. 4.

We will now proceed to execute a swinging movement.

With a Club in the right hand, assume the first position.

Carry the Club upward and backward to the position A, shown in the figure, which is the starting point of the movement.

Now swing it in the direction indicated by the dotted line, carrying it upward, forward, and sideway, to the position B, shown by the dotted Club. This movement is in front of the body, and backward to the left side.

Return the Club by the same sweep, as indicated by the arrows, B B B, to position A again.

Repeat the movement, and keep the arm extended as much as possible, assuming the attitude shown by the figure.

When fatigued with the right hand, change to the left.

This exercise will enable you to learn to balance yourself, and to become familiar with the weight of the Club.

FIGURE 4

Exercise No. 5.

This is a combination of the half Side and half Front Circles. They should be executed with the arms and Clubs fully extended.

Starting from the first position, (see figure,) raise them sideway and upward, in the direction indicated by the curved line and arrows, A B, until they reach the position shown by the dotted Clubs.

You have now described a half *Outer* Front Circle, with each hand.

Return them to the first position again, on the same line (A B) as indicated in the figure. This is the half *Inner* Front Circle.

Now carry them upward to the front, with the arms fully extended, following the direction indicated by the dotted lines in the figure, C. D. This is the half Outer Front Circle.

Return them to first position again, by the same line (C D.) This is the half Inner Front Circle.

The exercise may be varied, thus :

Raise the Club by the line A B, and return to first position by C D.

Endeavor to execute these movements fairly and smoothly, swinging the Clubs square to the front, and to the side on a line with the floor line.

46

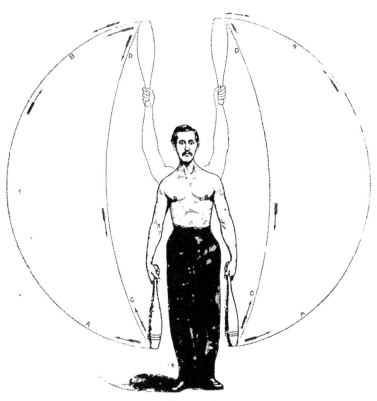

FIGURE 5.

Exercise No. 6.

This exercise is a combination of the half, Outer Back and half Outer Front Circles, involving rather an intricate change from one to the other.

From the first position, raise the Club in the right hand, horizontally, at arm's length, as shown in the figure.

Now let it fall backward and downward at the same time, bending the arm and somewhat relaxing the grasp, allowing it to describe the circle shown by the dotted line, A B C, arriving at the position indicated by the dotted Club, backward, over the head. This is a half Outer Back Circle.

Now change, and execute the half Outer Front Circle, by bringing the Club quickly forward, to clear the body well in front. When this is done, let it fall in the direction D E F, and carry it horizontally to A again, which is the half Outer Front Circle, and completes the movement.

Some difficulty will be experienced, at first, in executing this movement smoothly, but by noticing the natural turn of the arm, in executing the half Outer Back, you will master it after a few trials.

On arriving at the point C, bring the Club quickly forward, all in the same motion, ready to return it to the point A again by the half Outer Front.

Repeat until you can do it smoothly, before trying with the left hand.

Try and execute this movement double, simultaneously with the right and left hand, commencing with the Outer Back Circle by the right, simultaneously with the Outer Front Circle by the left, following with the Outer Back Circle by the left, simultaneously with the Outer Front Circle by the right.

FIGURE 6.

Exercise No. 7.

This is the Moulinet—so named from its resemblance to the movement in the broadsword exercise.

Starting from the second position, throw the Clubs forward, at arm's length, directly in front of the body, keeping them parallel, and apart about the width of the loins. Let them fall downward in the direction A, indicated in the figure, allowing them to turn freely between the thumb and forefinger, by relaxing the grasp. Bend the arms, closing the elbows in toward the body, and they will move easily in the direction shown in the figure, by the dotted Clubs.

Do not pause in the movement, but continue the circle in the direction B C, and repeat, endeavoring to get the peculiar twist of the wrist, and turn of the elbow, as perfect as possible.

It will be found, by a little practice, that the movement is not at all difficult, but depends on relaxing the grasp and throwing in the elbows at the proper time, that the circle may be described fairly and squarely, as indicated in the figure.

Endeavor to execute the Outer Moulinet with both Clubs, the direction of which is the exact reverse of this movement,

FIGURE 7

Exercise No. 8.

This exercise combines both the Inner and Outer Side Circles, complete.

From the first position, throw both Clubs forward and upward over the shoulders, into the position shown in the figure.

Now swing them together upward and forward again, following the dotted lines, in the direction indicated by the arrows, describing the complete circle A B C.

On carrying the Clubs backward to the point C, it will be found necessary to bend the body slightly forward, turning the palms of the hands upward. Keep the arms perfectly stiff and straight, and move the Clubs evenly together.

From the point C, reverse the movement, and carry them back again to the point A, as indicated in the figure.

These two movements are the Inner and Outer Side Circles—the first being the Inner, and the second the Outer.

In letting the Clubs fall backward, throw the chest out and well forward, carrying the elbows well back, and letting them fall as low as possible, hanging perpendicularly. Repeat until you do it well.

FIGURE 8.

Exercise No. 9.

This exercise is for the single Club, and you may take as heavy a one as you can use, or about double the weight of those used in pairs— say from ten to twenty pounds.

The dotted lines and arrows in the figure will explain the movement fully.

Start from the second position, at A, and carry the Club upward and over the shoulder to position B.

Next carry it up and forward, in the direction C D, and as far backward as E, returning it to the second position again, by the line F G H, as indicated by the arrows in the figure.

Assume the position shown by the figure, throwing the chest and shoulders forward.

Repeat the movement until fatigued, commencing with either arm, and alternating right and left.

FIGURE 9.

Exercise No. 10.

This is a combination of the Inner and Outer Moulinets with a half Inner and Outer Side Circle.

Commencing from the second position, (shown in the figure by the dotted Club,) carry the Clubs behind the shoulders, to the position given in the figure. From this point the movement commences, which is a very pretty one, and will require a little practice to execute it smoothly, particularly the Outer Moulinet. Move both Clubs together, and uniformly.

From the point A, swing both Clubs upward and forward, in the direction indicated by the line and arrows, A B C, and then describe a Front Moulinet, which will bring them round by the dotted line to D. Continue the movement in the direction D E, describing the half Inner Side Circle, which ends at F, and completes half the exercise.

Now return them in the direction G—on the same line—first describing a half Outer Side Circle, and then the reverse Moulinet, following the dotted line back to position A again.

The reverse of the Inner Moulinet will be found somewhat difficult, but a little patience and practice will master it.

Endeavor to execute the movements smoothly, with the Clubs together, and parallel, and apart sufficiently to clear the body nicely.

FIGURE 10.

Exercise No. 11.

This movement is a combination of the Inner and Outer Side Circles, the Inner being done with one arm, simultaneously with the Outer by the other.

From the first position, carry the Club in the right hand forward, and that in the left backward, as shown in the figure, the right describing a full Outer Side Circle, and the left a full Inner Side Circle, in the direction indicated by the arrows. The Clubs will pass each other, when perpendicularly above the head, and again when they reach the first position.

Next reverse the movement, changing the right hand to the Inner Side Circle, and the left to the Outer Side Circle.

In executing these movements, keep the arms fully extended, and swing the right uniformly with the left, passing the Clubs as above described. Turn the body from side to side, which you will find necessary to enable you to make a perfect circle.

FIGURE 11.

Exercise No. 12.

This movement, when well executed, is one of the most beautiful and graceful of the entire series. It is called the Horizontal—from the fact that, in the completion of the circles, or sweeps, at the point of a reverse of them, both Clubs are in a horizontal position; one directly above and behind the head, and the other at arm's length at the side, as seen in the figure.

This is called a simultaneous movement; the time of the movement of the right arm, in completing half the figure, is the same as that of the left, which is completing the other half. In this respect this exercise is somewhat similar to No. 6.

To fully understand the movement, we will go somewhat into details. Take at first a Club in the right hand, and carry it to position A, (see figure,) horizontally, over the head, and well backward, so that, when it falls, it will clear the head and shoulders well.

Now drop it, describing a half Inner Back Circle, in the direction of the backward line, A A A, (see figure,) at the same time straightening the arm and bringing the Club in a horizontal position, at arm's length, at the right side, as shown by the dotted arm in the figure.

Now bring the Club forward by the Front Outer Circle, following the front line, A A A, in the direction of the arrows, but instead of carrying it completely around, shorten the sweep by bending the arm, as it passes in front of the body, and carry it up and over the head again, to the position A, from whence it started, as shown in the figure.

Repeat this until you do it smoothly. Note the peculiar movement of carrying the Club quickly backward, as it passes over the head, to enable it to clear the head freely as it drops behind again.

Practice the left hand, the positions of which you can find by reference to the figure, they being relatively the same as the right.

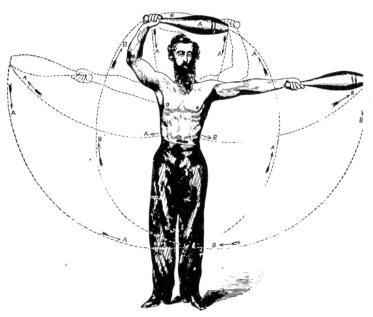

FIGURE 12.

Exercise No. 13.

This exercise is more difficult to describe than to execute. It is familiarly known as the "Windmill," from its resemblance to the four arms of a windmill following each other round and round, in one direction.

This beautiful figure comprises four distinct motions of the Alphabet, following each other successively, and alternating with the right and left arms; commencing first with the Inner Front, right arm; second, the Inner Back, left arm; third, the Outer Back, right arm; and fourth, the Outer Front, left arm; then repeating from the first again, *ad libitum*.

It will be noticed that all the circles are described in the same direction, and each Club closely following the other, gives the movement a similarity to the windmill, thus suggesting its appropriate name.

Take the second position. Commencing with the right hand, describe the Inner Front Circle, in the direction D E F, (see figure,) and at the moment it reaches the point F, start off with the left arm, in the direction D—indicated by the arrow—and describe an Inner Back Circle, D E F, (see figure,) which follow by the Outer Back with the right arm, which has got around in position to execute it. (See A B C, in figure.)

Immediately follow with the left again, which is at G, executing the Outer Front by the line G H I. (See figure.)

The time it takes to execute a Back Inner or Outer Circle being exactly the same as for an Outer or Inner Front Circle, by bearing this in mind, and commencing slowly to execute the four movements, in their respective turns as before explained—giving each its regular time, one, two, three, four—you will soon catch the movement, and find it very simple.

FIGURE 13.

Exercise No. 14.

This exercise is a variation of No. 13, and is similar in detail, differing only in carrying the Clubs together, in company, instead of alternately.

From the second position, raise the Clubs, as indicated in the figure, preparatory to executing simultaneously the Inner Back Circle with the right arm, and the Outer Back Circle with the left.

Let both Clubs fall together in the direction indicated by the arrows at A A and B B, each describing their respective Back Circles, and moving exactly together in the same direction, and coming around again to the position shown in the figure.

Now follow the lines C C, in the direction D D, with both Clubs in close company, describing with the right a Front Outer, and with the left a Front Inner Circle, again coming around to the position shown in the figure. Now the Inner Backs again, then the Fronts, and so on alternately, and you have the movement.

A variation of the direction of the movement to the right—a reverse of the above—completes this exercise.

Exercise No. 15.

This exercise is a combination of the Front and Back Circles, requiring a little practice and some skill in execution. It is a very fine, as well as difficult movement.

Be careful and avoid collision as the Clubs cross. It will be well to practice this movement at first with a very light Club.

By referring to the figure, it will be seen that the Clubs cross each other, near the hand, which is the secret of the movement, and when brought around to the position shown, bring the hands close together, that the point of crossing may be at the smallest part of the Club.

The apparent position of the Clubs, in the figure, is directly over the head, but they should be back far enough to clear the shoulders nicely.

Commence the movement with the Inner Back Circles, simultaneously with the right and left, and follow by the Inner Front Circles, repeating each alternately.

From the position given in the figure, let each Club fall downward, the one in the right hand following the dotted line, A B C D E, and the one in the left following the same line, in the reverse direction. The Clubs must, of course, cross each other, to get around together, both behind and in front, as indicated by the dotted lines in the figure.

In executing the Back Circles, make due allowance for the crossing of the Clubs, which may pass each other at either side. It is well, however, to practice passing them alternately, right and left, behind.

Learn to do the Back Circles well, before trying the combination of the Front.

FIGURE 15.

Exercise No. 16.

This exercise appears, from the figure, to be somewhat complicated and difficult, though it is comparatively easy and simple after you have mastered the two movements forming the combination, viz.: the Inner Back Circles simultaneously, (as in Exercise No. 15,) and the double Front Moulinet, (as in Exercise No. 7.)

Commencing from the second position, carry the Clubs to the position shown in the figure, preparatory to the execution of the Inner Back Circles.

On the completion of the Inner Back Circles, carry the Clubs forward, and together, in position to execute the forward Moulinet, as in Exercise No. 7. Then, with no pause in the movement, carry the Clubs upward and backward, as shown in the figure, and repeat alternately the two movements, *ad libitum.*

The dotted lines and arrows shown in the figure indicate the movement, but after you have become familiar with the different movements of the foregoing exercises, a written explanation will be as easily understood as a figure or diagram, and, in this case, more so.

EXERCISES FOR LADIES.

As a means of exercise, both pleasing and beneficial, there is nothing for ladies more suitable and simple than the Indian Clubs.

We append a few simple movements, only by way of introduction, for the reason that all of the foregoing exercises are just as well adapted for ladies as for gentlemen, though ladies, of course, should use lighter weights.

The weight for ladies is from three to five pounds. The dress should be loose, and the arms free to move in any position, and nothing to prevent a full expansion of the chest.

Many of the exercises can be executed with such skill and grace as to approach "the poetry of motion," and when accompanied by music they can be rendered pleasing accomplishments.

Half an hour with the Clubs, daily, divided morning and evening, will soon do away with much that is artificial about womankind, and promote the natural development of a graceful form and movement

Exercise No. 17.

Take the first position, as shown by the figure, the Clubs hanging pendant by the side.

Raise the right Club slowly in front, and to the left, in the direction indicated by the line A, carrying it to the position• B, as shown by the dotted arm and Club—holding it horizontally and directly over the head.

Retain it in this position for a few seconds, and then let it drop, by the same line, to the first position again.

Repeat this movement several times with the right, and then try the left arm, then the right and left alternately.

72

FIGURE 17

Exercise No. 18.

This exercise should be executed very slowly, and prolonged until it produces fatigue.

Raise the Clubs to the second position, as shown in the figure—the Clubs perpendicular, and the hands directly in front of and about the height of the shoulders.

Carry them slowly from B to C, fully extending the arms at the side, horizontally. Next return them, by the line D, to position B again.

Now carry them backward, by the line E, until they reach the position indicated by the dotted Clubs in the figure.

Raise them to the second position again, and repeat the movement. Do all this slowly, keeping the Clubs exactly perpendicular.

74

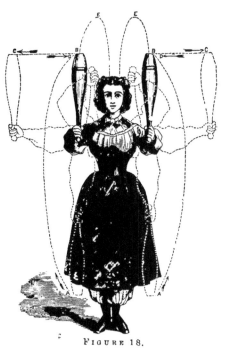

FIGURE 18.

Exercise No. 19.

This movement has already been fully described, in the preliminary exercises, as the Inner Back Circle.

From the second position, (see figure,) carry the Club in the right arm upward and backward over the head, letting it turn in the direction A, and falling, follow the line B C; after which, bring it back in front, to the second position again.

❧ Practice until you can do this smoothly.

Next try the left arm, and when perfect with that, alternate the right and left, in constant succession, with no pause in the movement.

FIGURE 19

Exercise No. 20.

This is the Front Moulinet, and has been fully described in the Alphabet.

This movement is particularly trying to the wrist, and tends to develop at part, which is proportionally weaker than any other part of the arm.

Start with a Club in the right hand, holding it in the second position.

Let it fall outwardly, and directly in front, in the direction A, as dicated in the figure, following the line B C, completing a perfect circle.

As the Club falls forward to the position B, the elbow must be closed toward the body, and the grasp somewhat relaxed, with the palm of the nd turned toward the body.

The foregoing instructions must be closely observed in this movement, :fore you can do it correctly.

When perfect with the right hand, try the left; then both together, and ternately.

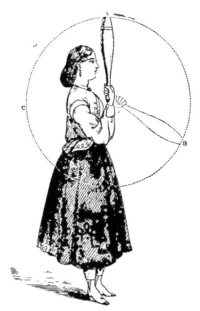

FIGURE 20

Printed in Great Britain
by Amazon